To the Nation For the Nation

RAJ KAPILA is Director and Chief Editor, Academic Foundation. An alumnus of Delhi School of Economics, he has been involved in journalism (early part of his career) and finally, publishing. Author/editor of several books, his special interests include economics, current affairs and issues concerning India's development.

To the Nation
For the Nation

Selections

from Selected Speeches of
Dr. Manmohan Singh

Compiled and edited by
Raj Kapila

ACADEMIC FOUNDATION
NEW DELHI

First published in 2006
by
ACADEMIC FOUNDATION
4772-73 / 23 Bharat Ram Road, (23 Ansari Road),
Darya Ganj, New Delhi - 110 002 (India).
Phones : 23245001 / 02 / 03 / 04.
Fax : +91-11-23245005.
E-mail : academic@vsnl.com
www.academicfoundation.com

To the Nation, For the Nation :
Selections from Selected Speeches by Dr. Manmohan Singh
compiled and edited by
Raj Kapila

ISBN 81-7188-543-8

Typeset and designed by Italics India, New Delhi

Printed and bound in India

CONTENTS

To the Nation, For the Nation

The idea of SELECTIONS from the selected speeches of Dr. Manmohan Singh, came to my mind when I read the concluding paragraphs of his first speech—his Address to the Nation,[1] in which he frankly stated: "When I chose to enter public life I did so because I was convinced that our democracy needs more professionals to become active in politics." He, therefore, appealed to all "to participate in public life so that governments at all levels—central, state and local—are constantly put on notice and not just tested once in five years." Dr. Manmohan Singh said: "Fellow citizens, I urge you to come forward and play an active role in the nation's public affairs. Each one of you can make a difference. I seek your support to restore to our public life a greater sense of purpose and a renewed commitment to decency, morality and hard work needed to take our country forward. We must re-capture the spirit of idealism and self-sacrifice which characterised the high noon of our freedom struggle."

1. On 24th June, 2004 after taking over as the Prime Minister under the United Progressive Alliance government.

But for another two months there was no speech from him except the one which had to be there on the Flag-hoisting occasion, 15th August, 2004, at the Red Fort—again an Address to the Nation—when he said: "I have no promises to make, but I have promises to keep." He went on to add: " The real challenge for me and for the Government at all levels is the challenge of implementation of our stated policies and programmes. Central, State and local bodies have to work together for Government to be an effective instrument of development for the benefit of our people."

After this, started the process of Prime Minister Manmohan Singh's speeches—a speech on every occasion in which he participated. Some words, phrases, and sentences are expressions of feelings coming from the core of his heart—expressions that bring out the simple and sincere, and profound truth uppermost in his mind. Let us say—from the core of his heart, and from the core of his mind...

New Delhi
January 11, 2006

—Raj Kapila

Time has come to make history...

There comes an occasion, though rarely, in the life of a nation when it can be said that the time has come to make history. We are today at the threshold of such an era.... Our political system and leadership must show sagacity, wisdom and foresight so that we are able to make the best of this moment and make India a truly great nation. An India where there are no barriers between the government and the people. An India where each and every Indian can stand proudly and proclaim that he is an Indian. Let us work together to build such a nation.

Prime Minister's Independence Day Address, New Delhi, 15th August, 2005.

At the cusp of a historic change

India, is at the cusp of a historic change in its economic history. It is possible for the economy to enter into a sustained phase of growth of 7-8%, breaking away from the trends of the recent past. The economy has already demostrated this capability and I am confident that this potential will be realised. Our manufacturing sector has shown tremendous dynamism and our services sector has been a key driver of growth. Hopefully, with our focus on agriculture and irrigation, the primary sectors too will show faster growth. Infrastructure is a constraint and requires huge investments in roads, railways, ports, power, civil aviation and telecommunications so that our growth processes are not throttled. With all round growth and with the possibilities thrown open by technological developments, it is possible for us to eradicate poverty and liberate our people from want, disease and ignorance within a decade. This is a feasible goal which we should aim for.

Prime Minister inaugurates Golden Jubilee Celebrations of LIC, Lucknow, 1st September, 2005.

India as an emerging power

It is not only we but the entire world is viewing India as an emerging power. The whole world is eagerly watching the manner in which India is making rapid economic progress. And this economic growth is happening within the framework of a liberal democracy. Our country is a multi-cultural, multi-religious, multi-lingual and multi-ethnic nation. Nowhere in the world do we have an example of a country of over 1000 million people seeking their economic and social destiny within the framework of a democracy. It is because of this that the entire world's attention is riveted on us. It is the result of our combined hard work that India today has made its mark on the world stage and we feel proud of our standing in the comity of nations.

Prime Minister's Independence Day Address, New Delhi, 15th August, 2005.

Confluence of civilizations

We have to inculcate liberalism in our people. Our educational system, our media, our popular culture must reinforce the civilizational commitment of India to pluralism and inclusiveness. Equally, our legislature, our judiciary, our executive must at all times be cognizant of this need to renew our commitment to the founding principles of our Republic and the guiding principles of our Constitution. Our Government is firmly wedded to these principles. We are committed to the social, political, economic and educational empowerment of scheduled castes, scheduled tribes, other backward classes, all minorities and all weaker sections of society, especially women. The empowerment of every section of society can only help empower our nation. Every group must necessarily see and have a stake in our collective success and prosperity.

Prime Minister's Address at the National Integration Council, New Delhi, 31st August, 2005.

The ideologies of communalism, of casteism, of regional and linguistic chauvinism have to be fought in a more sustained and intelligent manner. We need a more humane, inclusive and liberal political culture. Our social and family values must be rooted in our civilisational commitment to pluralism and liberalism. The idea of India, is the idea of *Vasudhaiva Kutumbakam*. The whole world is one family. The idea that even if nations may clash with one another, cultures and civilizations can co-exist. The defining feature of the 21st Century is not that it will be marked by a 'clash of civilizations', but that it will be shaped by a 'confluence of civilizations.'

The process of nation building

Our Nation is what we are. India will be what we make of ourselves. Our thoughts and actions will shape her. The efforts of millions of people go into the formation of a nation. The process of nation building is a great enterprise of adventure and creativity. It requires all of us to work together, bonded by our love for our Motherland. This love flows from our identity as Indians. Whatever be our religion, region, language, caste or culture, we are all Indians and India is ours. Our strength derives from our unity in diversity. The principles of secularism, social justice and the equality of all before law constitute the defining feature of our nation.[1]

In Nation building the involvement of millions of school children is essential. An aware child creates an aware household. An aware household can create an aware community. An aware community creates an aware Nation. The child is our starting point,

1. Prime Minister's Independence Day Address, New Delhi, 15th August, 2005.

the Nation the beneficiary. I have found from my own experience that children are these days shaping the thinking of their elders.[2]

Youth are the future of the nation. Educated and employed youth are a Nation's asset; uneducated or unemployed they can become a liability. We should, therefore, endeavour to provide employment opportunities so that people are not viewed as a liability but become an asset.[3]

---

2. Prime Minister's remarks at the Rajiv Gandhi Renewable Energy Day Function, 20th August, 2005.
3. Prime Minister's Address at the All India Congress Committee Session, New Delhi, 21st August, 2004.

A code of conduct for all political parties

The time has come for us to evolve a code of conduct for all political parties, a code of ethics for all individuals in public life, and a code of best practices for the Government at all levels.

We must look within our parties, and ourselves, and ask what is the root cause of the decline in values in public life? How do we reform our public institutions, our political parties, and our government at various levels?

Prime Minister's Independence Day Address, New Delhi, 15th August, 2004.

Larger concept of nationhood

The challenge of regionalism has a new dimension today that we must consciously address. Forty years ago, our political leadership was more conscious of the historical and political roots of regionalism, since our nation was still young. Over time, we have been able to address many of these political factors. However, there is a resurgence of regional and sub-regional identities in a manner which was not conceivable sixty years ago. As a pluralistic society and polity, we have adequate space for regional and sub-regional identities and cultures. These are not necessarily inimical to our larger concept of nationhood. Our Constitution gives a place of honour to all regional languages. Technological developments in communication, IT and media have made it possible for small communities and local cultures to preserve and

---

Prime Minister's Address at the National Integration Council, New Delhi, 31st August, 2005.

promote their unique identities in a manner inconceivable in the past. We must rejoice in the blossoming of these regional identities and lay emphasis on harmony rather than uniformity. We must at the same time ensure that these local identities become a part of our diverse mosaic in a harmonious way rather than become the cause for divisiveness and exclusion.

"Bharat Nirman"

It is not possible for our rural areas to develop in the absence of basic infrastructural facilities. In order to improve basic infrastructure in rural areas, we have conceived of an ambitious programme called *Bharat Nirman*. In *Bharat Nirman*, one crore hectares of unirrigated land will be irrigated. All villages whose population is 1000 or more, (and 500 or more in hilly areas) will be connected by roads. Two and a half crore houses will be given electricity connections, and through this, the entire country will be electrified, and every village will have at least one telephone connection.

Prime Minister's Independence Day Address, New Delhi, 15th August, 2005.

Young people in the 21st century

India will have the world's largest number of young people in the 21st Century. Are we doing enough to educate them to equip them intellectually so that every citizen becomes an economic asset and not a social liability? Are we doing enough to invest in the capabilities of our next generation—their health care, their employment opportunities, their leisure time activities? Are we doing enough to prepare our people for the strategic shifts happening in the world and the consequences for us in India!

Release of the Report "A Caring Government-One Year of UPA", New Delhi, 22nd May, 2005.

Desire to go to school

It is necessary for every section of society to be literate and educated. By strengthening *Sarva Shiksha Abhiyan*, we are trying to ensure universalisation of primary education. We are giving special emphasis to the education of the girl child. We need to make education joyful, interesting and meaningful so that children develop a desire to go to school. We are resolute in our commitment to see that no child is deprived of the benefit of primary education. It is our hope that in the near future, women are as literate as men. In order to achieve these goals, resources shall not be a constraint. We are also committed to providing education to disabled children as well.

Prime Minister's Independence Day Address, New Delhi, 15th August, 2005.

Attention to higher education

Along with primary education, we also need to pay attention to higher education. If India is seen around the world as a rising knowledge power, it is because of our Universities and Research Institutions. If we want to maintain our rapid economic growth, we need to improve the quality of these institutions and also create many more such institutions. Let us resolve to achieve excellence in academic work in the 150th anniversary year of the Universities of Kolkata, Mumbai and Chennai.

Prime Minister's Independence Day Address, New Delhi, 15th August, 2005.

Listen to the people

Let us all learn to listen to the people. What do they want? They want governments that are efficient, effective, transparent, honest and caring. They want a government that works. They want governments that will improve the quality of their life. They want leaders who know how to listen.

Prime Minister's Address at the All India Congress Committee, New Delhi, 21st August, 2004.

Participation of the common man

In all our economic programmes, our policy has been to ensure the participation of the common man, particularly of those in rural areas. They should feel that all programmes belong to them. Shri Rajiv Gandhi had dreamt of *Panchayati Raj* many years ago. Today, the district, *tehsil* and village *panchayats* have a major responsibility to discharge. Our Constitution has placed the responsibility on *panchayats*, not only of ensuring economic development but also delivering social justice. *Bharat Nirman* provides a unique opportunity to our *panchayats* to shoulder this immense responsibility by effectively implementing this programme. I am confident that *panchayats* will ensure that Bharat *Nirman* becomes a milestone in our development process.

Prime Minister's Independence Day Address, New Delhi, 15th August, 2005.

Bedrock of a functioning democracy

Law and order is fundamental to the existence of a functioning democracy and a civilized society. The Rule of Law is the bedrock of a modern economy. As the instrument for maintaining the rule of law, an efficient, effective and an accountable police administration is one of the most important institutions of the modern state.

Prime Minister's Address at the Superintendents of Police Conference, New Delhi, 1st September, 2005.

Still governed by the Police Act of 1861

The police system has evolved over the last one and a half century. It is still governed by the Police Act of 1861. At that time, when the police force was created, the sole consideration was of defending the establishment rather than providing sensitive and friendly policing to our people. The police forces were to serve the interests of rulers and not people. Times have changed since then. We are an independent and democratic nation which takes pride in its civil liberties, its rule of law and its judicial system. In such a framework as we are in today, there is a need to have in the police forces a managerial philosophy, a value system and an ethos in tune with the changing needs of our times.

Prime Minister's Address at the Superintendents of Police Conference, New Delhi, 1st September, 2005.

Building such a culture, I believe, is one of the most important challenges that all police officers must address on a priority basis. We need to ensure that police forces at all levels, and even more so at the grassroots, change from a feudal force to a democratic service. Police forces need to be seen as a friend of the citizen, someone in whom a common man should repose trust and faith.

Policing in the new urban milieu

Visible contrasts in lifestyles, rising expectations and the breakdown of traditional family structures may be contributing to increased urban violence. Today, about one-third of the population lives in urban areas—in 20 years time, probably 50 per cent of the population will be living in urban areas. The problem of policing in the new urban milieu is on the horizon. Something concrete will have to be done to grapple with the challenges of policing in the new metros and the urban areas that cannot be simply wished away.

Prime Minister's Address at the Superintendents of Police Conference, New Delhi, 1st September, 2005.

Government cannot be wished away

Governments cannot be wished away, especially in a developing country like ours where the government has an important role to play. The challenge for economic reform today is to breathe new life into government so that it can play a positive role.

What is government? Government comprises people's representatives and civil servants. The reform of government is, therefore, a reform of the way we, the elected representatives and officials, work in government. It is you, fellow citizens, as members of the civil society, who must mobilise your enormous resources in support of such reform.

Prime Minister's Independence Day Address, New Delhi, 15th August, 2004.

Essential forum for public debate

Parliament is a forum which is sacred and it must be our collective endeavour to ensure that we maximise its effectiveness. I request parties across the entire political spectrum to respect Parliament as an essential forum for public debate so that we can move forward in the task of nation building which is a common goal for one and all.

Prime Minister's Address to the Nation, New Delhi, 24th June, 2004.

Arbitrary transfers demoralise our administration

Frequent and arbitrary transfers of officials, demoralise our administration, and we have to find ways and means to deal with this pernicious phenomena. I am convinced that the onerous duties and responsibilities which our District Collectors and District Superintendents of Police are required to carry out, cannot be carried out when there is excessive uncertainty of tenure; arbitrary transfers take place causing great deal of mental anguish.

Prime Minister's Address at the Superintendents of Police Conference, New Delhi, 1st September, 2005.

Ours is a society which has rejoiced in its diversity

Ours is a society which has rejoiced in its diversity; in its ability to shelter an incredible range of thoughts, ideas and beliefs; in its acceptance of criticism and debate not just in public life but in matters of philosophy and beliefs. It is this wonderful open-mindedness which has enabled all religions of the world to find a place under the Indian sun.

Prime Minister's Address at the National Integration Council, New Delhi, 31st August, 2005.

A galaxy of great leaders

India was blessed to have had a galaxy of great leaders during its freedom struggle. Few nations in the world have seen within the span of a single lifetime leaders and intellectuals such as Mahatma Gandhi, Pandit Jawaharlal Nehru, Subhash Chandra Bose, Sardar Patel, Rabindranath Tagore, C.V. Raman and scores of others who illuminated our national discourse. Together, that generation of national leaders left behind a very important value. The idea of pluralism; the idea of inclusiveness; the idea of unity in diversity.

Prime Minister unveils statue of Pandit Nehru at JNU campus, New Delhi, 14th November, 2005.

Rise to their expectations and build a great nation

I recall that Vinoba Bhave was born in September, 1895, at the very time when Swami Vivekananda was addressing the World Parliament of Religions in Chicago. It was only a few years later that Mahatma Gandhi started his first *Satyagraha* in South Africa. One rarely comes across in the span of one generation such great personalities born in one country to serve the cause of mankind worldwide.

Few nations are blessed to have in such a short span of time such a galaxy of great men. India was truly blessed during the 20th Century to be home to so many great, forward-looking, liberal, progressive, socially committed leaders. We must, in this Century, rise to their expectations and build a great nation.

Prime Minister's remarks on visit to Vinoba Niketan, Trivandrum, 3rd September, 2005.

Positive expectations—positive outcomes

It is now possible, as never before, for us to visualise an India without poverty, without disease and without the scourge of extreme deprivation. There is an air of optimism and, as a believer in the ideas of Lord Keynes, I am convinced that 'positive expectations have a way of yielding positive outcomes.'

Prime Minister's Address at the India-EU Business Summit, New Delhi, 7th September, 2005.

The backbone of our country

Our maximum emphasis has to be on agriculture. Farmers are the backbone of our country and of our economy. It is the result of their tireless efforts that today, we do not have any shortage of foodgrains in our country. The entire country is grateful to them for this. However, we must admit that our economic growth has not yet fully reached every individual in our society. This is particularly true of our rural areas. The growth in agriculture has not been at the required pace. Even today, over 60 per cent of our population is dependent on agriculture.

Prime Minister's remarks on visit to Vinoba Niketan, Trivandrum, 3rd September, 2005.

In peace and harmony with nature

Ours is a society in which agriculture is a way of life. It is not just a source of income and livelihood but also a way of living in peace and harmony with nature. The bright colours, the melodious music and the hearty fare we associate with harvest festivals is a celebration of life itself. In many parts of our vast sub-continent, people come together through such festivals, cutting across ethnic, linguistic, religious and other boundaries. Our Government is deeply and sincerely committed to the welfare and well-being of our farmers, of our workers and of all those who are engaged in building an India of our dreams. I do believe that by the end of our tenure in office we will create a new environment of economic security and prosperity for our farmers and all those engaged in productive activity. This requires new investment in rural India.

Prime Minister assures new investment in Rural India, New Delhi, 12th January, 2006.

Growth of our agricultural sector has not kept pace with our needs

In the last decade, the growth of our agricultural sector has not kept pace with either our needs or our legitimate ambitions. If our economy has to grow at 7-8 per cent per annum, and it must do so if we have to eliminate poverty within the next decade, agriculture too must demonstrate a growth rate of about 4 per cent per annum. For this to happen, there has to be a major improvement in our agricultural production practices. There has to be greater commitment to innovation in the technologies that are brought to bear in farming and an enhancement in the investments being made in the entire agricultural production chain. This requires, and that's inevitable, growing monetisation and growing commercialisation of the agricultural economy, perhaps, at a pace never thought of before. As our agricultural system gets commercialised, with

---

Prime Minister's speech at the Chief Minister's Conference on Revival of Co-operative Credit Structure, New Delhi, 9th September, 2005.

increasing participation of farmers in markets not only for agricultural products but also for agricultural inputs, farming starts taking on a new commercial and economic meaning. In such a scenario, and I dare say that such a transformation of our agriculture is essential, easy availability of agricultural credit has a very important influence on agricultural production, on agricultural investment and on technological upgradation of our agriculture. Therefore, we need–and we need it urgently–to put in place a credit delivery system that is equal to the challenges that our agricultural economy faces.

Cooperatives have failed but cooperatives must succeed

Cooperatives may not have delivered as per our expectations but they need to be revitalised and made effective. I recall in the early 50s Prof. D.R. Gadgil presided over a path-breaking report on rural credit and the theme of that report was–'Cooperatives have failed but cooperatives must succeed'. I think that theme is as relevant today as it was then, if India's rural economy is to measure up to the challenge of its regeneration and revitalisation.

The National Common Minimum Programme places significant emphasis not only on enhancing rural credit but also revitalising the cooperative sector. We had set an ambitious target last year of doubling agricultural credit flow in three years and we are on target so far. However, much more needs to be done. We need to ensure that the proportion of investment credit increases

---

Prime Minister's speech at the Chief Minister's Conference on Revival of Co-operative Credit Structure, New Delhi, 9th September, 2005.

even as agricultural credit rises. We need to ensure that the needs of small and marginal farmers, who are even more dependent on informal sources of credit, are met through the institutional credit system so that they can be rescued from the clutches of the traditional village moneylender.

Cooperatives are today at the crossroads. In many States we only have cooperatives in name, with very little stake-holder participation in their management. There have been no elections held for years. Government officials and ministers at the State level run the affairs of many of these so called cooperatives. There is no proper audit, little accountability often and poor governance. This state of affairs must change and must change rapidly. Of course, there are States in which the cooperatives are thriving. They should set an example for others to follow. The report of the Task Force has suggested a roadmap for revitalising the cooperative credit set up. It is built around a revival package for cleaning up their balance sheets and recapitalising them; on capacity building and qualitative improvement of personnel in the system; on institutional restructuring; and last but not least, on improving the regulatory regime within which the cooperative credit system has to function if it is to flourish in years to come. I believe that Chief Ministers should pay greater attention to these issues. What is important is that all the elements should be seen as a combined package rather than as separate, disparate elements to be chosen or dropped individually.

I also agree with the view expressed by the Task Force that any finanacial restructuring without addressing the root causes of the persistent weaknesses of the cooperatives would not result in a sustained revival of the cooperative credit system. Specific legal measures therefore, need to be taken to enable cooperatives to evolve into genuinely democratic, self-governing and financially well-managed institutions. The Task force has correctly recommended that any approach to the financial restructuring of cooperatives should be contingent on a commitment on their part and on the part of State Governments to the implementation of legal and institutional reforms.

Mahatma Gandhi endorsed our democratic heritage

India is proud of its democratic heritage which is rooted in the country's cultural ethos of tolerance, respect for different view-points and a ready embrace of diversity. Mahatma Gandhi led us into a non-violence struggle not only to free India from colonial rule but also to ensure to our people the exercise of their democratic rights. To him it was clear that the end to colonial rule would mean very little unless the broad masses of the people of India were empowered with democracy.

Our experience of more than 50 years of democratic rule demonstrates how democracy is a most powerful tool to successfully overcome the challenge of development. But most of all, democracy alone gives the assurance that the developmental aspirations of the poorest citizens of our society will be taken into consideration. This, above all, is the unique strength of a democratic system.

Prime Minister's remarks at the launching of UN Democracy Fund, New York, 14th September, 2005.

The culture of democracy

Democracy is a powerful ideal, but its successful exercise requires strong and enduring institutions, laws and procedures and the development of a parliamentary culture, whose essence is the accountability of those in authority to the ordinary citizens of the country, a strong and independent judiciary, a free press, professional civil and military establishments, constitutionally empowered institutions to safeguard the rights of minorities, of women and children and an independent electoral mechanism. The culture of democracy or the democratic temperament must be imbibed by citizens from a very early age. They must become aware of both their rights as individuals, but also their responsibilities and obligations as citizens.

Prime Minister's remarks at the launching of UN Democracy Fund, New York, 14th September, 2005.

The role of media

Good journalism should advocate the cause of the mute masses fairly and temperately. It should represent public opinion and create and educate such opinion. It should steer itself clear of any particular class, creed or party line and champion the cause of the people and should resolve to speak against class interests in case they clashed with the welfare of the masses. It should stand for the people and should make journalism an instrument of service to the people.

I have always believed in the importance of a free press. It is the ultimate check against the tyranny of authority. We are proud of our media and its contribution in shaping public opinion for nation building and social change. The high standards of

---

Prime Minister's speech at the Silver Jubilee event of the Chandigarh Press Club, Chandigarh, 24th September, 2005.

journalism prevailing in our country, in spite of the commercial pressures on media, testify to the robust traditions of independent journalism. Our free press has emerged as an important guarantor of democratic and human rights. Our media has given voice to the voiceless. It has ensured that every minority and marginal group is heard, is seen, is involved in the mainstream.

Media has been described as the last line of defence for freedom and democracy. Media holds a mirror to society. It constitutes an early warning system. Its assessments on numerous policies alert the nation to the prevailing situation and signal us to be mindful of the future challenges and opportunities.

To shape public opinion

In a democracy public opinion is, of course, the final arbiter. However, social scientists have a professional obligation, a social responsibility, to shape public opinion. They must intervene in public policy debates, especially at the local and community level, and guide both policymakers and the general public, so that informed choices are made. We live in a knowledge based world and policy choices must be based on knowledge.

I urge our research institutions to address vital issues of the day so that the political leadership in the country is better informed, so that our public debates are better informed, so that the choices we make, and the demands we make are better informed. While purely subjective and emotional issues do rise to the surface in any public campaign, researchers and analysts can play a vital role by enabling more informed, more reasoned and more mature discussion.

Prime Minister's speech at the Silver Jubilee of CESS, Hyderabad, 7th January, 2006.

Major religions of the world are represented in India

Globalisation has made the world so inter-dependent that none of us can ignore what happens elsewhere. Peace and prosperity are more indivisible than ever before in human history.

Indian democracy has been fashioned around India's civilizational ethos which celebrates diversity. Our society today is the culmination of centuries of assimilation of diverse peoples and ethnic groups. All the major religions of the world are represented in India. We have a tremendous diversity of languages, customs and traditions.

Prime Minister's Address to Joint Session of the Congress, Washington, 19th July, 2005.

Constitutionally mandated elections

The Father of our Nation, Mahatma Gandhi called for universal adult franchise as early as 1931, long before India became independent. Our political leadership remained true to this commitment. Over the past six decades, governments in India, at both the national and state level, have regularly sought the mandate of the people through elections.

The Constitution was amended to ensure constitutionally mandated elections to village and municipal councils. This process has produced no less than 30 lakh elected representatives in the country, with 10 lakh positions reserved for women. This has brought democracy closer to the people and also empowered women and promoted gender balance.

Prime Minister's Address to Joint Session of the Congress, Washington, 19th July, 2005.

The 21st century will be an Asian century

I do believe that the 21st century will be an Asian century and India must have a major role in making it happen. I have a vision of Asia in which India has to play a key role—a vision of a resurgent Asia; an Asia of inclusive societies and open markets; an Asia of enterprise and creativity, driven by knowledge and shaped by family values; an Asia of peace, stability and development; and a modern, secular and prosperous Asia.

Prime Minister's speech at the FICCI Annual Meeting, New Delhi, 24th December, 2005.

Rural India deserves better

A large part of the effort to build a better future for our people will have to be in our rural areas for the foreseeable future. No region of India can claim that the quality of life in its villages is satisfactory. Be it sanitation, be it drinking water, be it electricity and roads, be it education and health, be it public spaces and environment—whatever be the criterion, rural India deserves better.

The growth process of the last century has left village India far behind our big cities. This divide must not widen any further. The physical and social infrastructure in rural India must catch up with at least semi-urban India within the next decade.

Prime Minister's speech at the HT Leadership Summit, New Delhi, 15th November, 2005.

One of the world's biggest growth stories

Our task of development, of modernisation, will never acquire its true meaning and significance if our rural areas are not active partners in process of social and economic change. The economic and social development in our rural areas is going to be one of the world's biggest growth stories in the coming decade. A change in the way incomes are earned, the way incomes are spent, the way lives will be lived and livelihoods pursued. Over the last few years, we have been watching a makeover of Indian business in bridging the so-called divide between India and *Bharat.* Many firms have tried to capture rural opportunities and in the process they have opened up unprecedented possibilities for rural India to get more integrated with the national and global economy, where corporate India is connecting with the growth potential in rural India. This movement needs a quantum jump.

Prime Minister's speech at the CII conference on Bharat Nirman, New Delhi, 16th December, 2005.

Vision of a modern rural India

In 1976, Indira Gandhi had said at the Science Congress, and I quote: "The overwhelming majority of our people live in villages and will continue to do so for years to come. I would go further and say that we don't even want to uproot them. All over the world, urbanisation has brought comfort and stimulation; but who could claim that it has not given rise to complicated problems? Rural life should be so enriched as to prevent the migration of people and resources from villages to towns."

Indiraji's wise words ring true even today. Our strategy for rural India has to be one of improving the quality of life in village India, based on easily accessible and appropriate technologies, so that people can continue to live where their forefathers have for generations and yet live comfortable and decent lives.

Mahatma Gandhi once said: "If the village perishes, India perishes too."

Prime Minister's Address at the 93rd Session of Indian Science Congress, Hyderabad, 3rd January, 2006.

My vision of rural India is of a modern agrarian, industrial and services economy co-existing side by side, where people can live in well-equipped villages and commute easily to work, be it on the farm or in the non-farm economy. There is much that modern science and technology can do to realise this vision. Rural incomes have to be increased. Rural infrastructure has to be improved. Rural health and education needs to be met. Employment opportunities have to be created in rural areas.

All advanced agricultural economies are knowledge-based economies. We must broaden the knowledge base of our farmers to enable them to make the best use of new technologies. Our farmers' needs for information are multi-faceted and these are not limited to technology alone. They need information about agriculture as a business, about farming practices, about policy initiatives, about best practices of other farmers and on market intelligence. Therefore, timely availability of information is a critical component in the development of our agriculture.

While the share of agriculture in national income is falling rapidly, the share of population dependent on agriculture is not declining as rapidly. This is creating rural distress and contributing to enforced migration to urban areas. The only sensible response to this trend is to create productive employment opportunities in rural areas, both in the farm and non-farm sectors. We must develop labour-using technologies both in agriculture and in rural manufacturing so that jobs can be created closer home for those of our citizens who live in villages.

We have to encourage people living in rural areas to continue to live there even as the quality of their life is improved and more and more modern amenities are provided for them.

Private enterprise in the transformation of agriculture

I see immense opportunities for private enterprise in the transformation of agriculture. There are opportunities both for supplying inputs and for processing and marketing the agricultural produce. Agricultural growth is slowly responding to our incentives and if we sustain our efforts, we may see India becoming a new granary of the world. The private sector must not miss out on this opportunity and must ride the boom that I see now on the horizon.

Prime Minister's speech at the India Economic Summit, New Delhi, 29th Novembe , 2005.

Indian economy has now become more open

The Indian economy has now become more open, more globally integrated and more competitive. The seekers of protection then, line up now seeking greater openness. Truly, times have changed; mindsets have changed; attitudes have changed; aspirations have changed; and our hopes for the future have also changed. Our industry and enterprise are far more confident, competitive and ambitious about their future and they feel that they are second to none.

When the UPA government came to office in June 2004, there were worries about the direction of our policies. There were worries that the economy may falter and that we may sacrifice fiscal stability. I think we have proved that the policies of the UPA government are growth-friendly. Over the past 18 months, policies

---

Prime Minister's speech at the India Economic Summit, New Delhi, 29th November, 2005.

relating to investment, taxation, external trade, banking and finance, foreign direct investment, capital markets and small scale industries, have all evolved towards making our industry and enterprises more efficient, more globally competitive and as free from restrictions as possible.

The estimates of many economic think-tanks predict that we are likely to average 7.5 per cent growth rate per annum in the next four years. This is impressive in itself and is based on current policies. It is certainly within the realm of possibility that an appropriate combination of policies can raise this beyond 8 per cent easily. In fact, we should be targeting a 10 per cent growth rate in 2-3 years time. In my view, this is eminently feasible.

Our cities need a better future

Urban areas are focal centres for economic activity and their needs must be attended to on a priority basis. Our cities, which shelter a third of our population need a better future. The speed at which urbanisation is now taking place, the day is not far off when over 50 per cent of India's population will be residing in urban areas. Urban areas are the nodes from which enterprise, creativity and prosperity radiate in all directions. They are the engines of sustained growth that can absorb the millions of people who need to be gainfully employed outside agriculture. They need infrastructure, which is world class, infrastructure, which can cater to the needs of a rising population, infrastructure that can propel industrial and economic growth.

Prime Minister's speech at the India Economic Summit, New Delhi, 29th November, 2005.

New generations of the workforce

We have to create close to ten million jobs every year for the next few years to meet the demand for jobs that new generations of the workforce will seek. Most of these jobs will be sought by unskilled labour. We have therefore, to create employment opportunities for them in infrastructure, in manufacturing, in trade and transport. These jobs will be created only if we make it attractive for investors to invest in labour-absorbing technologies and labour-using sectors.

Prime Minister's speech at the India Economic Summit, New Delhi, 29th November, 2005.

Working class: The blood that flows through our veins

Our national movement recognised, from the very inception, the central role of the working class in national development. The working class is like the blood that flows through our veins. Our economy, our society, our nation functions because of the toil and energy of the working people of our country. Let there be no doubt about our commitment to the critical role of our working classes in carrying forward the process of social and economic change.

The ultimate security for all working people lies in the assurance of sustained economic growth and development. A country like ours has enormous potential for the growth of employment opportunities.

We cannot live with a jobless growth. We need growth, which will be employment friendly, we need growth which will create a lot more jobs in the process of social and economic change.

Prime Minister Addresses 40th Indian Labour Conference, New Delhi, 9th December, 2005.

We need new laws for new times. Laws which provide safety standards, which cater to the basic needs of workers, which take care of their welfare, which are flexible enough to create rather than destroy jobs, which increase the overall well-being of our people and particularly, the working people.

Appropriate and relevant labour legislation is in the interests of labour and in the interests of the nation as a whole. I urge our labour leaders and those committed to the welfare of the working class to recognise the reality.

If our manufacturing base has to grow, if employment opportunities have to be created, we must make our labour laws less rigid.

A path-breaking legislation

When we became independent, our Founding Fathers dreamt of a country where every citizen would be free from poverty, ignorance and disease—problems which had plagued millions of our people for centuries. While we have made remarkable progress in many spheres since then, it is still a matter of serious concern that large segments of our society still suffer from these age old scourges. It is only by empowering people and by granting them an inalienable right to a livelihood, can we ensure that such intentions and dreams get translated into reality.

In this context, the National Rural Employment Guarantee Act is a path-breaking legislation. It is a landmark in the economic history of our people, in the regime of rights enjoyed by our people, and in our efforts for social equity and justice. It entitles

---

Prime Minister's speech at Rural Development Ministers Meet, New Delhi, 27th September, 2005.

our rural poor to guaranteed employment, to a means of sustenance, a means to avert distress, a means to secure two square meals a day, and a means to lift them out of the trap of poverty.

The legal guarantee of 100 days of employment in a year to a rural household is unprecedented. India has set an example that I am sure many other countries will follow.

An economic superpower

In the long run, if growth is not to splinter our society, we must invest in the skill base of our people and in adequate social safety nets for the less well-off and deprived citizens of our ancient land. We have ambitions of being an economic superpower. This cannot be on a base where half our people are literate; where people do not have access to basic health facilities; where people do not have incomes in times of distress. In the long run, we must carry everyone along on this road to national prosperity. This is our vision for India. This must be your vision for India too.

Prime Minister's speech at the India Economic Summit, New Delhi, 29th November, 2005.

A revolution of rising expectations

Today, there is a revolution of rising expectations sweeping throughout Asia. We now face the choice of choosing between the path of inclusive, pluralistic and participatory development, and between more exclusionist models of development. Nations such as ours have consciously opted to be inclusive societies and open economies. We want to ensure that every one of our citizens leads a life of prosperity and dignity. Given the inevitability of globalisation. I do believe that all nations must deal with the challenge of pluralism as well. The message of unity in diversity is one that our societies offer to the world at large.

Prime Minister's Introductory remarks at the Jawaharlal Nehru Memorial Lecture, New Delhi, 21th November, 2005.

Building a better future

Through all known history, mankind has pursued little else than fulfillment of the desire for a better future. It is this constant dissatisfaction with the status quo that drives change, innovation, enterprise and progress. In the developing world, there are material reasons for such dissatisfaction. It is often suggested that we in India are culturally conditioned to accept a sub-optimal material existence because many of us seek greater happiness from non-material aspects of life. Even so, it can be nobody's case that we do not have to worry about our material standards of living.

Building a better future requires us to provide education for all, to provide access to better health facilities, to provide adequate housing and sanitation, to provide a liveable environment in villages and cities.

Prime Minister's speech at the HT Leadership Summit, New Delhi, 15th November, 2005.

Urban areas are the nodes

Urban areas are the nodes from which enterprise, creativity and prosperity radiate in all directions. They are the engine of sustained growth that can absorb the millions of people who need to be gainfully employed outside agriculture. However, today our cities are often unable to meet the basic needs of their residents on many counts. They need infrastructure which is world class, infrastructure which can cater to the needs of a rising population, infrastructure that can propel industrial and economic growth. While a National Urban Renewal Mission is being launched to meet the infrastructure needs, I sincerely believe that we need a new wave of city building for the 21st century. Empires of the past rejoiced in establishing new cities. We need to create new cities which can cater to a much larger urban population, cities which will be a tribute to our current times.

Prime Minister's speech at the HT Leadership Summit, New Delhi, 15th November, 2005.

New investments in the world class public infrastructure

Our cities cannot continue to develop in the manner in which they have done over the past few decades. We urgently need new investments in world class public infrastructure for our cities. Delhi Metro has already improved the quality of life of our citizens in the Nation's capital. Our cities have to become more livable and more people-friendly. We have to also take steps to enable people who work in the city to be able to live away from it thereby contributing to efforts underway to decongest. All this can be possible only with rapid public transport. As the population of a city grows, the importance of public transport increases. In the absence of good, reliable and affordable public transport, private vehicles will dominate the roads leading to congestion, pollution, more accidents and of course, more fuel consumption.

Prime Minister Inaugurates Dwarka Metro Line, New Delhi, 30th December, 2005.

Delhi Metro is an example of one of the most technologically advanced and safe, rail based mass transit systems in the world. Although capital intensive, metros have a case for them in high traffic intensity situations. I am sure the citizens of other cities like Bangalore, Hyderabad, Mumbai, Ahmedabad and Kochi are looking forward to this kind of facility.

Urbanisation is a relentless process

There is no doubt that India by and large still lives in our villages. But the development process of the past five decades has made a significant difference. An increasing share of our population now lives in urban India. Urbanisation is a relentless process, which has come to stay and has to be factored into all our developmental thinking and development processes. We have already added 65 million persons to our urban population in the decade of the '90s alone. We are poised to have nearly 50 per cent of India living in our cities by the earlier part of the present century and that should give an idea of the magnitude of the development and renewal task that awaits all of us.

Prime Minister launches Jawaharlal Nehru National Urban Renewal Mission, New Delhi, 3rd December, 2005.

Restoring our historical glory

Let us not forget that in the history of the world, Indians stood out as city builders as evident from the traditions we carry from the ancient civilizations of Harappa and Mohenjadaro. Those cities were symbols of human engineering excellence in their own times. We should work to make them come alive again through this Mission: Jawaharlal Nehru National Urban Renewal Mission. I have great pleasure in launching the Mission. Like many Indians living in our cities, I look forward to it with great hope.

Prime Minister launches Jawaharlal Nehru National Urban Renewal Mission, New Delhi, 3rd December, 2005.

Ready to take on the world

There are many Indians who are ready to take on the world, to compete globally, to test their skills and sell their wares on the global stage. We have to enable them to realise their full potential. We must not prevent the full flowering of the creativity, enterprise and talent of our professionals, our entrepreneurs, our artists and our skilled workers. In the past we shackled them with rules and regulations. Regrettably, in many areas, we continue to do so even today.

I sincerely believe that most Indians want to be actively engaged in the global economy, as indeed they have been for centuries. Indians live, work and prosper on all continents of the world.

A nation of over a billion people is destined to be an active participant in the intellectual, cultural, political and economic transactions of the 21st century.

Prime Minister's speech at the HT Leadership Summit, New Delhi, 15th November, 2005.

Most important elements of our globalisation

To my mind, the most important aspect of re-connecting with the world is for us to reach out to the People of Indian Origin. The NRIs and the PIOs are the most important elements of our globalisation. There is a fundamental difference between the globalisation of India and many other developing countries. For us, globalisation is a natural means of linking up with the international community of Indians. As I said last year, if there is one phenomenon in the world over which the sun truly never sets, it is the phenomenon of the global community of people of Indian origin.

Prime Minister's speech at the Pravasi Bharatiya Diwas 2006, Hyderabad, 7th January, 2006.

India is a land of opportunity

On the 4th Pravasi Bharatiya Diwas 2006, I may state that: India is a land of opportunity that places premium on enterprise and creativity. Our Government is committed to create a hospitable climate for investment and enterprise. We will work hard to improve the quality of governance at all levels, and remove barriers to growth and competition. I invite you to make use of the investment and business opportunities that India offers. I invite you to be active partners of a new India and walk with us in finding new pathways of development and progress. I invite you to feel the love and affection of Mother India and feel the warmth of her embrace.

Prime Minister's speech at the Pravasi Bharatiya Diwas 2006, Hyderabad, 7th January, 2006.

Quality of governance

No government can sustain a social safety net unless the economy grows at a reasonable pace and generates the required revenues. Hence, fiscal sustainability of growth is an important pre-requisite for a more equitable growth process. Bankrupt governments cannot promote equity, leave alone growth. An improvement in the quality of governance can create a virtuous cycle of rising investment, rising employment, rising incomes and rising growth.

Prime Minister's speech at the Silver Jubilee of CESS, Hyderabad, 7th January, 2006.

Inter-regional economic imbalances

One of the drivers of divisive regional identities has been the persistence of regional economic imbalances. They remain and may have even increased. Even though it is true that all regions of the country are today generally better off than 40 years ago, some regions have developed at a faster pace than others. Relative inter-regional disparities are a problem that must be addressed. This is not just in the interests of national integration but also in the interest of the welfare of our people. I urge the Chief Ministers from the less developed States to learn from the example of the more developed ones and find new pathways of progress for the people of their region.

Prime Minister's Address at the National Integration Council, New Delhi, 31st August, 2005.

Inter-regional variations in growth and development

The subject of inter-regional variations in development has engaged economists in India for a long time. Several factors combine to influence inter-regional variations in growth and development. The extent of agrarian transformation, pace of urbanisation, the quality of infrastructure, level of human resources development, and the quality of overall governance are all important determinants of regional variations in development. Since a large proportion of our population is still dependent on agriculture, differences in the rates of growth of agricultural output and productivity are bound to be an important factor contributing to regional disparities in the level of development and standard of living.

Prime Minister's speech at the Silver Jubilee of CESS, Hyderabad, 7th January, 2006.

A study of these aspects of development can contribute a great deal to our understanding of regional inequalities. What factors are inhibiting development in the more backward areas of our country? Will political decentralisation and administrative unbundling help or hinder the development of less developed regions? What are the relative roles of the State and Markets in enabling development?

Woman, the unquestioned leader

We must feel truly proud of the fact that our national movement did have a very positive impact on the status of women. The women and men who came together were deeply influenced by the teachings and example of Mahatma Gandhi. Gandhiji was perhaps the first political leader anywhere in the world to draw ordinary women out of the household, out of the kitchen, out of their seclusion and into public life, onto the streets and on the political stage. Few national movements anywhere in the world had so many women participating in them in such large numbers, so spontaneously.

Reflecting on his 25 years in public life in 1940, Gandhiji observed, and I quote: "My contribution lies in my presenting for acceptance 'truth and *ahimsa*' in every walk of life, whether for individuals or nations. I have hugged the hope that in this, woman

---

Prime Minister's speech at the Celebration of Golden Jubilee of Andhra Yuvathi Mandali's Sisu Vihar School, Hyderabad, 7th January, 2006.

will be the unquestioned leader and, having thus found her place in human evolution, will shed her inferiority complex. Woman is the incarnation of *ahimsa*. *Ahimsa* means infinite love, which again means infinite capacity for suffering. And who but woman, the mother of man, shows this capacity in the largest measure? Let her translate that love to the whole of humanity... and she will occupy her proud position by the side of man. She can become the leader in *satyagraha*."

Rise of a major free trade area in Asia

I am certain that in the next few years, we may see the rise of a major free trade area in Asia covering all major Asian economies: India, including China, Japan and South Korea and possibly extending to Australia and New Zealand. This Pan-Asian Free Trade Area could be the third pole of the world economy after the European Union and North Atlantic Free Trade Area and will, I am certain, open up new growth avenues for our own economy.

Prime Minister's speech at the India Economic Summit, New Delhi, 29th November, 2005.

United Nations awaits a 'New Deal'

The United Nations today suffers from a democracy deficit. Its structure and decision-making processes reflect the world of 1945, not the world of the year 2005-06.

India has a special regard for the United Nations. The ideals of the UN run parallel to our own civilizational ethos. The UN is the ancient Indian concept of '*Vasudhaiva Kutumbakam*' or 'the whole world is one family'. It is this idea of a shared destiny, which encouraged the UN Assembly, five years ago, to adopt the Millennium Development Goals.

The United Nations today is in need of urgent and comprehensive reforms. It must include the expansion of the United Nations Security Council in both permanent and non-permanent categories of membership.

Prime Minister's Address at the 60th session of the UN General Assembly, New York, 15th September, 2005.

The world awaits a 'New Deal' that can spur development and create jobs on a global scale. It must address the challenge of eradicating mass poverty.

In this 'One World' there is only One United Nations. If we fail the United Nations, we will fail succeeding generations, who will expect a more enlightened legacy than is currently in sight. Globalisation offers exciting opportunities to improve living standards world-wide provided the weak and the powerless are empowered to become genuine partners in progress. The world community must therefore, muster the courage to harness the potential of globalisation for the benefit of entire humankind.

In 1947, India's first Prime Minister Jawaharlal Nehru said, "Peace has been said to be indivisible; so is freedom, so is prosperity, and so also is disaster in this One World that can no longer be split into isolated fragments." Today, these words assume a compelling logic.

Unique category of literature

Any literature that captures the beauty and finer aspects of life in the midst of gloom and despondency is truly a great literature. Munshi Premchand's writings belong to that unique category of literature which have deeply influenced progressive forces all over the world. While dealings with the pain and agony of common people under foreign rule, his writings focus attention on the powerful current of nationalism which eventually shook the foundation of the British Empire and brought us our independence.

Prime Minister's speech on the release of Munshi Premchand's books, New Delhi, 10th January, 2006.

'The Great Pravasi'

On the Pravasi Bharatiya Diwas last year we met in Mumbai. We met in the port city at which the "Great Pravasi", Mahatma Gandhi, arrived 91 years ago, returning to his Motherland from South Africa. He returned to liberate our country from the colonial yoke. He returned to inspire us, to guide us, to forge a new unity in our ancient land... The leader of the South African people, Mr. Ahmed Kathrada, fought, as Gandhiji did, to free his people and to lead them into a brave new world of freedom, dignity and self-respect. The people of Indian origin have come to symbolise the world over, the spirit of a free people, of a people who have the courage to stand on their own two feet. A people who have time and again demonstrated the power of unity amidst diversity, of knowledge and compassion over force and authority. Our civilization is based on the idea of plurality, diversity, tolerance, and on the possibility of the co-existence of multiple identities.

Prime Minister's speech at the Pravasi Bharatiya Diwas 2006, Hyderabad, 7th January, 2006.